# How People Lived in America
# Toys, Games, and Fun in American History

by Dana Meachen Rau

Reading consultant:
Susan Nations, M.Ed.,
author/literacy coach/
consultant in literacy development

**Please visit our web site at: www.garethstevens.com**
For a free color catalog describing Weekly Reader® Early Learning Library's list
of high-quality books, call 1-800-542-2595 (USA) or 1-800-387-3178 (Canada).
Gareth Stevens Publishing's fax: (877) 542-2596

**Library of Congress Cataloging-in-Publication Data**

Rau, Dana Meachen, 1971-
    Toys, games, and fun in American history / by Dana Meachen Rau.
      p. cm. — (How people lived in America)
    Includes bibliographical references and index.
    ISBN-10: 0-8368-7209-6  ISBN-13: 978-0-8368-7209-5 (lib. bdg.)
    ISBN-10: 0-8368-7216-9  ISBN-13: 978-0-8368-7216-3 (softcover)
    1. Toys—United States—History—Juvenile literature.  2. Games—United States—History—
Juvenile literature.  3. Amusements—United States—History—Juvenile literature.  I. Title.
    GV1218.5.R38  2007
    790.1'33'—dc22
                                                        2006008636

Copyright © 2007 by Gareth Stevens Publishing

Editor: Barbara Kiely Miller
Art direction: Tammy West
Cover design and page layout: Kami Strunsee
Picture research: Sabrina Crewe

Picture credits: Cover, title page, pp. 14, 18 © Bettmann/CORBIS; p. 4 © Bob Daemmrich/
PhotoEdit; pp. 6, 7, 8, 9, 12, 16, 19, 20 The Granger Collection, New York; pp. 10, 13
© North Wind Picture Archives; p. 11 National Museum of American History, Smithsonian
Institution, Behring Center; p. 15 Library of Congress; p. 17 © Museum of History and
Industry/CORBIS; p. 21 © William Gottlieb/CORBIS

Printed in the United States of America

1 2 3 4 5 6 7 8 9 10 09 08 07

# Table of Contents

Having Fun Today . . . . . . . . . . . . . . . . . . . . . . . . . . .4

Fun in Early America . . . . . . . . . . . . . . . . . . . . .6

New Things to See and Do . . . . . . . . . . . . . . . . . .11

Playing and Watching Sports . . . . . . . . . . . . . . .16

Pictures and Sound . . . . . . . . . . . . . . . . . . . .19

Glossary . . . . . . . . . . . . . . . . . . . . . . . . . . . .22

For More Information . . . . . . . . . . . . . . . . . .23

Index . . . . . . . . . . . . . . . . . . . . . . . . . . . . . .24

Cover: Sledding on snow has always been fun. In 1900, these children in New York sledded in Central Park.

Some video games are so small they can be played anywhere.

## Having Fun Today

Today, people play **video** games with sounds and flashing lights. People who lived long ago did not have these kinds of games. But some games have been around for hundreds of years. The first **settlers** who came to America played cards, dice, and hopscotch. People have always tried to find ways to have fun!

## Long ago, people . . .

- did not have video and computer games;
- did not have toy cars;
- did not have action figures;
- did not have radios or televisions;
- did not watch movies;
- did not watch games between sports teams;
- did not play soccer;
- did not take vacations;
- did not play on playgrounds.

5

Settlers had only a few small tools to help pick their crops.

Many settlers came to America about four hundred years ago. These early Americans did not have much time to play. They worked hard. They had to find and grow food. They had to take care of their animals and homes. From morning to night, people always had work to do.

The settlers found ways to make their **chores** more fun. Men and boys liked to hunt and fish together. Men helped each other with bigger jobs. They worked together to clear trees from fields or build a new barn.

A group of men could build a barn in only a couple of days. They had fun working as a team.

Women of all ages came to quilting bees. The women could work and visit with their friends at the same time.

Women met to sew **quilts**. Their gatherings were called **quilting bees**. A quilt is a blanket made from sewing together small **scraps** of cloth. While they sewed, the women talked and shared stories with each other.

Children had some homemade toys. They rolled wooden **hoops** by pushing them along with a stick. They raced their hoops to a finish line. Some children made marbles from balls of clay or round pebbles. Girls played with dolls made out of **cornhusks** or rags.

Boys played simple games outside with wooden hoops or paddles.

Children liked being active. They walked on stilts, bowled, and swung from trees.

After school, children had a little time to play outside. They played hopscotch by jumping on squares they drew in the dirt with a stick. They played leapfrog by jumping over each other like frogs. In winter, they skated on frozen ponds. They rode wooden sleds down steep, snowy hills.

# New Things to See and Do

In the early 1800s, not many toys were made in the United States. Some people ordered toys from other countries. These toys cost a lot of money. In 1840, an American company started making dolls. By the late 1800s and early 1900s, more and more toys were made in the United States.

This doll is one of the first kinds of dolls made in the United States.

Rich people were able to buy toys for their children. The toys were kept in a nursery.

Some homes had a room called a **nursery**. It was a room just for children and held all their toys. Girls played with paper dolls, tea sets, and dollhouses there. Boys played with toy soldiers and toy trains. Many toys moved by turning a key to wind them up.

New machines were **invented** in the late 1800s. They changed the kinds of jobs people could do. Many people moved from farms to cities. They started to work in **factories**. They no longer had to work every day from morning to night. After a busy week at a factory job, people had time off to have fun.

People enjoyed walking in parks on their days off from work.

13

Everyone in a family enjoyed going to the beach. The swimsuits they wore covered up most of their bodies.

Many families took summer **vacations**. Some families went to the seashore or the mountains. Cities built playgrounds for children to play on. Cities used some land for parks, too. Families went to the parks to play and have picnics.

Many people visited Coney Island in New York. They went to its **amusement park**. They played games and rode the roller coaster. People in many cities went to the circus. The Barnum and Bailey Circus traveled to small and large cities by train. The circus set up a big tent. It put on a show with clowns, wild animals, and **acrobats**.

Both adults and children liked to visit Coney Island.
This amusement park had many famous rides

Women had to ride bikes while wearing long skirts.

# Playing and Watching Sports

People started to play more sports. People who lived in America played tennis for the first time in 1874. They started to ride bicycles, too. Both men and women took long rides together. Some bikes were made for two or more riders!

All during the 1800s, people played baseball. This sport was also called townball. Teams from nearby towns played each other. People started coming to watch their games. By the late 1800s, teams from cities all over the country were playing each other.

Boys liked to play baseball. They wanted to be like the ball players they heard about in the news.

In 1903, two baseball teams played in the first **World Series**. Thousands of fans watched the Boston Pilgrims beat the Pittsburgh Pirates. African American players did not play in the World Series. They were not allowed on the same teams as white players. It was not until 1947 that black and white players could play baseball together!

Jackie Robinson played for the Brooklyn Dodgers. He was the first black player to join an all-white baseball team.

People had watched stories acted out in plays for hundreds of years.  But in the early 1900s, they could see stories on a movie screen.  The first movies were only about ten minutes long.  They had no sound.  Movies with sound came out in the 1920s.  People loved going to huge, fancy theaters to watch movies.  Children enjoyed cartoons made by Walt Disney.

Movie theaters had piano players. They played during movies that did not have sound.

19

This ad shows the kinds of TVs people could buy in the 1950s.

In the early 1900s, families often sat around radios in their homes. They listened to radio shows. The shows were on for hours every night. By the 1950s, people started buying TVs. The first TV screens were small, and the pictures were in black and white. Soon, screens were made bigger. Programs were shown in color. Families watched sports, news, and weekly TV shows for adults and children.

People who live in America today are different from people who lived long ago. We have different jobs and chores. We play with different toys and go different places. But one thing has stayed the same. People have always found ways to have fun!

These boys playing leapfrog show that children do not need toys to have fun. They just need each other!

# Glossary

**acrobats** — people who can do tricks with their bodies

**amusement park** — a park where people can play games, go on rides such as a merry-go-round, and buy food and drinks

**chores** — jobs around a house or farm that need to be done on a regular basis, such as every day or every week

**cornhusks** — the outer part of ears of corn

**factories** — places where workers make or put together goods other people can use

**hoops** — circular bands used to hold the sides of barrels together, or large circular rings

**invented** — to think up and make something new that no one has made before

**quilts** — blankets made of many scraps of cloth that are sewn to a second piece of cloth with a soft layer in between them.

**scraps** — left over pieces of material

**settlers** — people who move to and develop a new area

**World Series** — the yearly championship that is played to find out which is the best professional baseball team in North America

# For More Information

## Books

*Leagues Apart: The Men and Times of the Negro Baseball Leagues.* Lawrence S. Ritter (HarperTrophy)

*Quilting Now & Then.* Karen B. Willing (Now & Then Publications)

*Schoolyard Games.* Historic Communities (series). Bobbie Kalman (Crabtree Publishing)

## Web Site

The History Channel: History of Toys and Games
*www.historychannel.com/exhibits/toys/*
Learn about the history of some toys and games and their inventors. Explore a toy timeline and take a quiz on toys.

**Publisher's note to educators and parents:** Our editors have carefully reviewed this Web site to ensure that it is suitable for children. Many Web sites change frequently, however, and we cannot guarantee that a site's future contents will continue to meet our high standards of quality and educational value. Be advised that children should be closely supervised whenever they access the Internet.

# Index

amusement parks 15

baseball 17, 18

bicycles 16

boys 7, 9, 12

circuses 15

Coney Island 15

dolls 9, 11

early settlers 6, 7

games 4, 5, 10

girls 9, 12

making toys 9, 11

movies 5, 19

nurseries 12

outdoor games 10

parks 13, 14, 15

playgrounds 14

quilting bees 8

radios 20

roller coasters 15

sledding 10

sports 5, 16, 17, 18

televisions 5, 20

toys 5, 9, 11, 12

vacations 5, 14

video games 4, 5

## About the Author

**Dana Meachen Rau** is the author of more than one hundred and fifty children's books, including nonfiction and books for early readers. She writes about history, science, geography, people, and even toys! She lives with her family in Burlington, Connecticut.